To Kerry
C. S.

To Mark, Finn, Rudy, and Teddy
T. H.

Text copyright © 2018 by Claire Saxby
Illustrations copyright © 2018 by Tannya Harricks

First U.S. edition 2019

Library of Congress Catalog Card Number pending
ISBN 978-0-7636-9886-7

APS 23 22 21 20 19 18
10 9 8 7 6 5 4 3 2 1

Printed in Humen, Dongguan, China

This book was typeset in Avenir Next and Berkeley.
The illustrations were done in oil paint.

Candlewick Press
99 Dover Street
Somerville, Massachusetts 02144

visit us at www.candlewick.com

DINGO

CLAIRE SAXBY

ILLUSTRATED BY
TANNYA HARRICKS

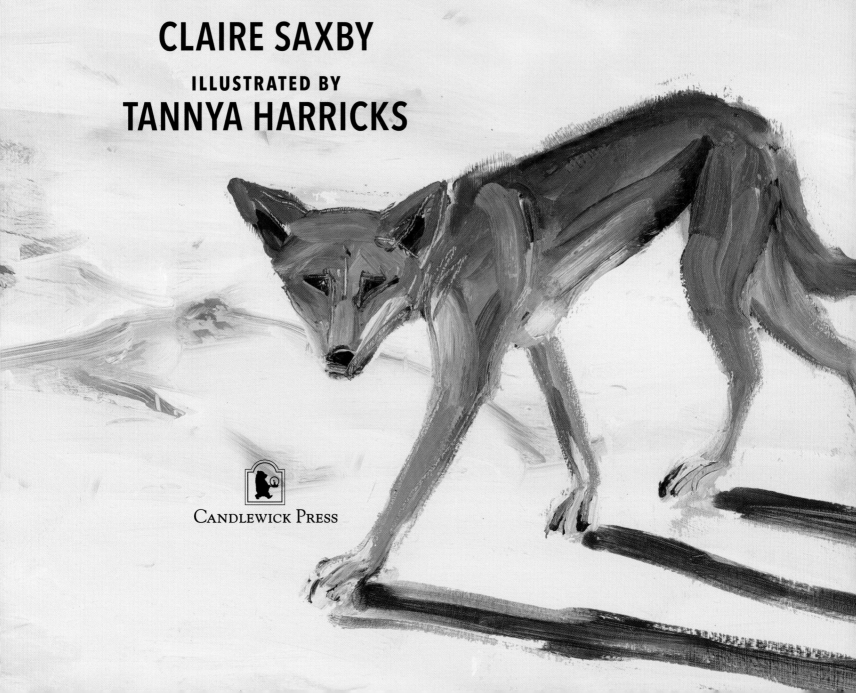

CANDLEWICK PRESS

Can you see her?

There—deep in the stretching shadows—a dingo.
Her pointed ears twitch.
Her tawny eyes flash in the low-slung sun.

Dingoes are most active at dusk and dawn.
In hot climates, they are almost nocturnal,
but in cooler areas, they may hunt throughout the day.

Dingo lifts her head, tastes the air, then uncurls.
Five plump pups spill onto the ground.
They are nine weeks old and recently weaned.

The rest of the pack still sleeps.
Dingo nudges the dozy pups toward her mate, and they
curl back into sleep.

A pack, like a family, can be small or large, ranging from two to twelve members.
All pack members help to raise the pups. Young independent males may live alone
or form a loose pack with other males until they find their own mate.

Dingo listens.
Dusk is a busy time.
Dusk is the time for hunting.

Many of Australia's forest animals are nocturnal, sleeping through the day and waking at dusk.

13

Dingo runs softly, softly through the forest.
She is sure-footed, flexible, and fast.

Dingo footpads are larger than those of dogs of a similar size, and their joints are more mobile. Dingoes are lean and can travel up to 25 miles/40 kilometers per day.

Can you see what she sees?
Possum climbs too high.
Wombat burrows too deep.

Dingoes need a lot of energy, so their main diet is meat, but they will also eat insects, eggs, and some plants.

Lizard is slow in the cool evening.

Too slow.

Dingo sniffs the air, then sniffs the ground
and follows the scent she finds there.
Can you smell what she smells?
In the gully. Kangaroos.
They are too big for Dingo to catch alone.
She travels on.

Dingoes are clever and determined hunters. They hunt alone or in packs, depending on the size of the prey.

She climbs to the highest point
and snuffs into the wind.
Rabbits!

A snuff is a strong out-breath and is
thought to allow a bigger in-breath,
which helps dingoes detect prey.
Their sense of smell is up to 100 times
better than that of humans.

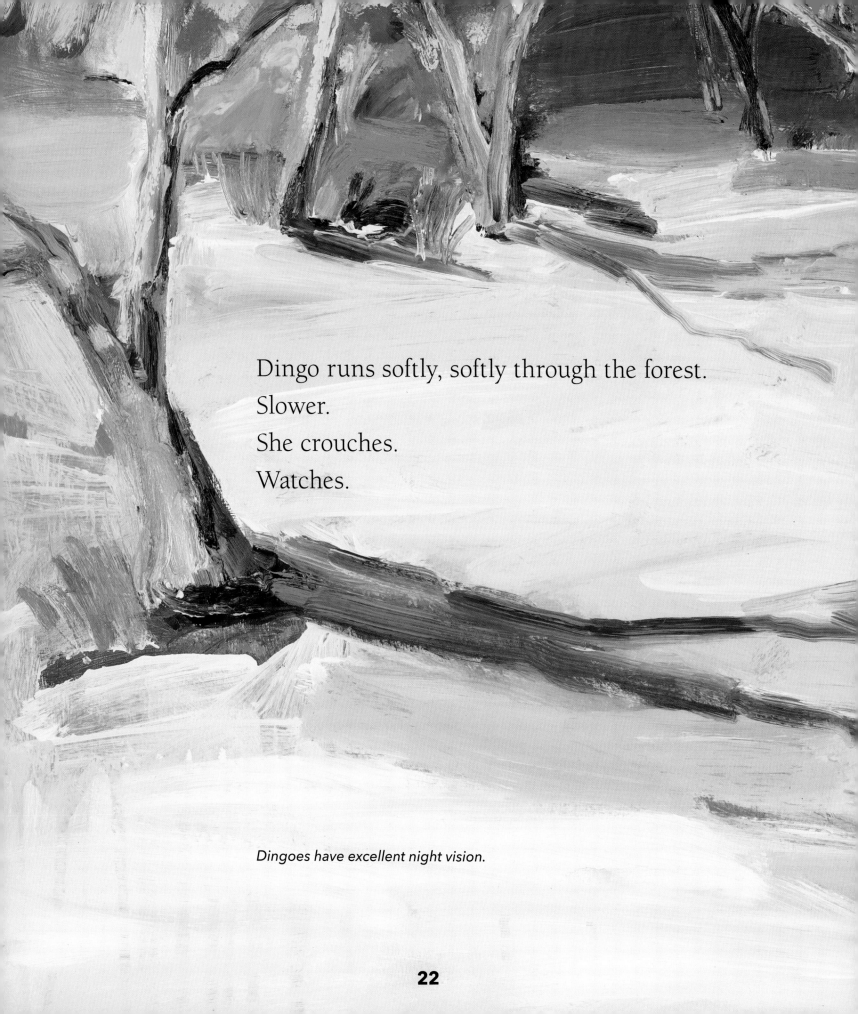

Dingo runs softly, softly through the forest.
Slower.
She crouches.
Watches.

Dingoes have excellent night vision.

Almost before the rabbit sees her, she has it.
Dingo carries her prize back to the den.
A frenzy of golden pups greets her.

The pups are growing fast, ever-hungry.
One day soon, they will join the hunt.
But not tonight.
Tonight they will stay here,
safe in their rocky den.

When the pack hunts, one dingo will stay behind to protect the pups. Dingo pups are usually three to four months old before they can run with the pack.

After a short rest, Dingo sniffs the air and,
with her mate, melts into the night.
They run through the forest, close but not together.
The night is young, and there is hunting to be done.

Dingoes have a variety of howl-calls to talk to one another and warn of danger.

Though you look, you may not see her.
Though you listen, you may not hear her.

Dingo moves softly, softly through the forest.

INFORMATION ABOUT DINGOES

Dingoes make their homes across Australia in a variety of habitats, from red deserts to alpine forests. They have lived in Australia for many thousands of years. They are a medium-size member of the dog family but are much more flexible than domestic dogs. Their skull is the widest part of their body, so if they can get their head through an opening, the rest of their body will be able to pass through too. Their packs have well-defined hierarchies, and generally only the dominant pair has pups. Dingoes are top-order predators; habitat destruction by humans is the biggest threat to their population.